LINKEDI... MARKETING

Use LinkedIn B2B Marketing to Generate Qualified Prospects and Obtain Clients

BOOK DESCRIPTION

LinkedIn is the world's largest professional network platform. With over 500 million professionally-connected members, this is a giant opportunity for your Business-to-Business (B2B) marketing. This book guides you on how to use LinkedIn B2B marketing to generate qualified prospects and obtain clients.

To appreciate what awaits you should you take up LinkedIn advertising, this guide begins by providing you with proven benefits of LinkedIn advertising so that you may know your gains well in advance.

While LinkedIn has been used successfully by many companies to market their businesses, it is not a one-platform-fits-all kind of basket. There are those types of business that have a higher potential to gain from the uniqueness of LinkedIn platform and there are those that have a lower potential of deriving the same gain. This simply means that LinkedIn must be evaluated on a case-to-case basis. In this guide, you will find valuable criteria that will enable you to determine whether LinkedIn suits your marketing needs or not so that you do not risk your resources against potentially low ROI (return on investment).

Professionals like belonging to clubs. Online, groups are the equivalent of professional clubs. Thus, you need to know how to use LinkedIn groups to your marketing advantage. This guide will show you how you can leverage the power of groups to gain a competitive edge in your niche.

LinkedIn Ads are quite unique from other forms of online Ads. This means that you have to give them special attention by learning how to effectively use them for maximum results. We are going to show you how to use the various types of LinkedIn Ads to increase your income flow.

What is the benefit of having a large following without an impact on your revenue? None! Most enterprises make the mistake of working so hard to acquire a huge following on LinkedIn without knowing how to financially gain from this following. We provide you with practical approaches to grow and monetize your LinkedIn following so that you can increase your income.

Finally, there is a limit to how much you can do as an individual. Even if you employ a dozen more people to work specifically on your LinkedIn account, you cannot completely tap into the huge potential base of over 500 million people. This is where automation comes in handy. Technologies exist that can help you to effortlessly automate your LinkedIn income. This guide provides you with information on how you can automate your LinkedIn income and the specific tools you require in order to harness great success.

Kindly download or print this book to learn more.

Enjoy your reading!

GIFT INCLUDED

If you are an entrepreneur, an aspiring entrepreneur, someone who is trying to create additional income stream or even someone who just loves self-improvement books; then you need to read my recommendations for top 10 business books ever. These books read by me have changed my life for the better.

Top 10 Business Books

ABOUT THE AUTHOR

George Pain is an entrepreneur, author and business consultant. He specializes in setting up online businesses from scratch, investment income strategies and global mobility solutions. He has successfully built several businesses from the ground up and is excited to share his knowledge with you.

DISCLAIMER

CONTENTS

INTRODUCTION

Social media networks have become a great source of potential leads. LinkedIn is one such social media network. However, unlike other social media networks, LinkedIn is a dedicated professional network characterized by members who are successful professionals, leaders in their respective companies, industries, and fields. LinkedIn has become such a marketing goldmine for Business-to-Business (B2B) companies. You too should not be left behind in digging up this goldmine. We have prepared this guide to help you take a vantage position in mining this great opportunity.

The practical information provided in this guide shows you how to use LinkedIn B2B marketing to generate qualified prospects and obtain clients. You will learn how to grow and effectively monetize your LinkedIn following. You will also learn how to scale-up your income flow through automation so that how much you earn is not constrained by limited human resource capacity but rather advanced forward by technology.

Keep reading to learn more.

BENEFITS OF LINKEDIN ADVERTISING

LinkedIn has the highest saturation of professionals and enterprise decision-makers. This makes it unique compared to other social media networks. Thus, your advert is more likely to reach the targeted audience for business than any other network.

The following are some of the benefits of LinkedIn advertising:

1. It is highly targeted

With such a high concentration of professionals, executives and business leaders, this makes the best place to expose your B2B (Business-to-Business) advert.

2. It is well-suited for B2B advertising

Generally, LinkedIn is not suitable for B2C (Business-to-Consumer) kind of advertising. This is where other social media do well. However, LinkedIn is unrivaled when it comes to B2B targeting. With LinkedIn, your advert is more likely going to grab attention of the eyes of the companies' top captains than on other social networks.

3. A great variety of ads to choose from

LinkedIn has a unique form of advertising compared to other social media. Its advertising features are highly personalized for a professional touch. Besides that, they are plenty of options to choose from that suit your particular needs. As we shall see later under the section "How to Use LinkedIn Ads", there are a variety of unique Ad types not found in any other social media.

4. Easy connection with influencers

LinkedIn has 61 million high influencers. The biggest advantage is that most of them are professional influencers. As such, they are highly likely to connect with you if your business aligns with their professional needs. They are not the highly aggressive types that are in for monetary inducements.

5. Long-form content marketing

Unlike other social media, LinkedIn provides an opportunity for long-form content marketing. Long-form content allows you to dwell deeper into your brand and make your audience have an incisive perspective. Since most of the people on the LinkedIn are professionals, they are more adept at such content as it enables them to understand your company and brand much better.

6. Better SEO

According to Hubspot study, LinkedIn does well on SERP (Search Engine Results Page) placements as a network that delivers the best improvement in search rankings per activity. Thus, you are more likely to get traffic to your web page from LinkedIn activity than from any other social media activity.

7. Leveraging LinkedIn groups for your adverts

Most of the highly impactful business activities take place within LinkedIn groups. It is from these groups that you are able to gain personalized professional touch. LinkedIn groups are good for content marketing. Thus, you can use your posts and discussions in LinkedIn groups to advertise your brand in the subtlest way yet experience a much better outcome.

8. Reach out to high-income professionals

LinkedIn demographic has a high concentration of senior professionals who range in the 30-59-year age bracket and an average income of $75,000 per year. Not only are a significant number of them in positions capable of making B2B purchase decisions, but they too have higher purchasing power for consumption. This means that if you are dealing with high-end consumer products and services, you are more likely going to receive a better response.

9. Filters for advanced targeting to industry-specific variables

LinkedIn focuses on industry-specific variables for targeting audience. Such variables include;

- Industry
- Company size
- Company name
- Skill
- Degree type and name
- Seniority
- Job function
- Job title

These parameters are highly suitable for B2B targeting. They are also good for B2C targeting when it comes to offering professional opportunities such as recruitment.

10. High-level lead nurturing capabilities

LinkedIn has Lead Accelerator feature. This feature allows one to track high net-worth prospects and precisely target them. It also offers opportunities for list-based advertising and remarketing to recent web visitors. All these features help to nurture leads on their journey to becoming customers.

11. Set own campaign

LinkedIn has a self-serve interface that allows one to easily setup own advertising campaign without requiring external help. This makes it easy for small-scale business without an adequate budget to higher specialists to do this on their own. Nonetheless, self-serve features are more elaborate and more advanced such that regardless of the firm size, the purpose is well served.

12. Get the 'right' clicks

LinkedIn high-precision parameters make it easy to get the right high-value clicks rather than plenty of low-value clicks with a low viability of conversion. It is better to get fewer clicks that convert than so many clicks that hardly convert. If your campaign is based on CPC, then, this guarantees you high ROI on your investment.

13. Higher conversion rates

With the right audience, advanced filtering, specialized lead nurturing and focus on the right clicks, you are guaranteed higher conversion rates compared to other social media networks.

IS LINKEDIN ADVERTISING RIGHT FOR YOU?

As we have stated earlier, although LinkedIn can be used for B2C targeting, it is highly suitable for B2B targeting. That should be your first criteria for determining whether LinkedIn is right for you or not. However, there are always exceptions to any rule. For example, if you are rendering professional services, executive training services, car loans, mortgages, and such other services and products that professionals would love to buy, then, B2C can work for you. Nonetheless, the B2C products and services to offer are quite narrow.

To understand if LinkedIn Advertising is right for you, let us have a look at what the statistics are saying.

Info statistics:

- 94% of B2B Marketers use LinkedIn to distribute content. [Source: LinkedIn Business]
- 80% of B2B leads come from LinkedIn. [Source: LinkedIn Business]

- 79% of marketers consider LinkedIn as a potential source of B2B lead generation. [Source: LinkedIn Business]
- Over 70% of LinkedIn members are outside the United States. [Source: LinkedIn Business]
- 57% of LinkedIn visitors access it via mobile phones. [Source: LinkedIn Business]
- 46% of social media traffic to B2B Company sites comes from LinkedIn. [Source: LinkedIn Business]
- 43% of marketers claim to have sourced a customer from LinkedIn. [Source: LinkedIn Business]
- Before a buy decision is made, decision-makers consume about 10 pieces of content from a given source. [Source: LinkedIn Business]

From the statistics, you can see clearly that LinkedIn is more cut out for B2B endeavors than B2C endeavors. With 80% of B2B traffic flowing from LinkedIn which has just about 100 million active members per month compared to Facebook that has about 1 billion active members per month, not forgetting Twitter, Instagram, Snapchat and others highly popular social media networks combined, it simply means that LinkedIn is highly focused on B2B.

If you are in the B2B sector, then, this is a full endorsement. However, you will need to consider several other factors before conclusively establishing that LinkedIn is where you ought to be.

Such factors include:

- Target customers
- Target audience
- Competitor activity
- Budget

Target customers

Though there are more professionals on LinkedIn than other social media networks, the target customers are mostly enterprises. However, these enterprises can only be represented by individuals; the professionals, CEOs, and other decision-makers. In fact, 41% of Fortune 500 CEOs are on LinkedIn. Thus, if you are targeting one or several of the Fortune 500 companies, LinkedIn is the right place to find their representatives.

Target audience

Targeting audience on LinkedIn is not a wild-goose chase. Thus, you not only need to target the right audience but also must be knowledgeable about them. The more precise you are about your target audience the higher the ROI you can derive from each target.

If you are targeting highly educated professionals, then LinkedIn is the right platform for you. Knowing the following will guide you in refining your target:

1. Know your target audience's job titles. This is important if you are offering customized service to an audience within a specific title. For example, if your organization is to facilitate audit assistants to become certified, then, you will filter out to get all those who have the title 'Audit Assistants' and target your ads to them.

2. Know the workplace of your target audience. There are occasions where you want to target a certain corporation, yet you do not have direct connections. The best way is to use LinkedIn filters to get employees working for that company and target them with your ads. This could be for job hunting or probably advertising certain equipment that can suit their needs.

3. Know the roles played by your target audience. This is important when it comes to decision-making. The more senior the target audience, the more likely they are going to influence decisions regarding your advert.

4. Know the unique skills and interests of your target audience. Knowing your target audience skills and interests is extremely important. These are things that they hold close to their hearts. Having a product or service that requires a particular skill to handle or advances a

particular skill or interest will more likely result in a better response to your ad.

Competitor activity

If you are in the B2B sector, know that your competitors are more likely going to be on LinkedIn than any other social media. This is supported by the statistics, which shows that 94% of B2B marketers use LinkedIn to distribute their content. Why not you? Furthermore, 79% of marketers view LinkedIn as the best place to source B2B leads.

If you do not want to be left behind by your competitors or you would like to be able to monitor and match up with their activity, then, you are better off being on LinkedIn.

Budget

Advertising on LinkedIn costs several times more than advertising on other social media networks. This is primarily because of a small number of highly targeted audiences. This raises competition by B2B advertisers for the opportunity to reach out to this niche.

According to AdStage, the following were LinkedIn average figures for advertising in 2017:

- Average CPM for LinkedIn Ads was $8.39
- Average CPC for LinkedIn Ads was $6.50
- Average CTR for the LinkedIn Ad was 0.13%

You must factor these Ad rates into your budget. A small B2B company should be more conscious of how these rates could deeply impact on its marketing budget and the likelihood of it not being a better way to optimize its marketing ROI.

Who should advertise on LinkedIn

Generally, the following are the most potent areas to be advertised or considered on LinkedIn:

- High-value B2B products and services
- Recruiting efforts
- Higher Education

High-value B2B products and services

In case you are offering high-value B2B products and services such as subscription services e.g. SaaS, then you are likely going to hit big on your LinkedIn advertising.

Recruiting efforts

If you are HR Consultant or company seeking high-level professionals, LinkedIn is the place to have the most impactful advert. With advanced filtering mechanism, such as education level, professional level, years of experience, and salary level, job title, age, among others, you can easily target specific potentials and are likely going to get the right kind of staff.

Higher education

If you are an institution of higher learning and offer an advanced degree program; for example, masters, doctorate, or executive degree programs, then targeting those with at least a bachelor's degree will be the most appropriate thing to do.

On the other hand, you could be a large university with huge alumni. You want to connect with your alumni for particular academic and social programs such as sponsorships, then, targeting those who attended your particular institution of higher education would yield optimal impact.

Who should not be advertising on LinkedIn

LinkedIn is not suitable for all kinds of advertising. Thus, there are those advertisers who may not get adequate ROI for their advertising campaign due to the unique nature of the LinkedIn audience. The following are some of the entities that should weigh their position well before considering advertising on LinkedIn:

- B2C companies – These are better served by other social media networks such as Facebook and Twitter. This is primarily because LinkedIn does not have such targeting parameters that you can use to target your audience. Furthermore, the cost of clicks on LinkedIn is several times higher than that of Facebook and Twitter, which makes it poor for ROI on small-scale sales.

- Smaller deal sizes – As a rule of thumb, for a deal that is lower than $10,000, it is more costly to use LinkedIn as you may spend more on ads than your gains.

- Broad targets – LinkedIn is for a specific target. If you are targeting broad base (such as gender, or age), then it is better to use other social media channels.

- E-commerce – Ecommerce is ideal for 'buy-now' CTAs. However, most of LinkedIn audiences are not inclined to such as they attend the platform to network.

- Commodities – Commodities generally fetch lower CTR (Click-Through Rate) on LinkedIn. It may seem appealing to offer high-end commodities such as bank loans, real estate, and insurance policy, among others. However, most of the professionals on LinkedIn are already networked with contacts offering such services. However, there is a chance to harness young professionals who are just entering the trade.

Advantages of LinkedIn Advertising

Advertising on LinkedIn has certain unique benefits. The following are some of the benefits you gain by advertising on LinkedIn:

- A broad variety of ad types – As we have seen before, LinkedIn provides a broad range of unique Ad types. This helps you to package your Ad in the most effective manner.
- Targeting precision – Due to its advanced filtering options, you can have more specific targeting which yields higher ROI
- Specialized analytics tools – With advanced tracking and analytics tools, you can easily measure the performance of your Ad campaign in terms of lead generation, conversion rate, and ROI
- Flexible budget – With LinkedIn, there is neither minimum nor maximum cost when it comes to advertising. You can create your own customized budget and finance your campaign as much as you can.

USING LINKEDIN GROUPS

LinkedIn groups are the most powerful of any group on social media network in terms of professional competence. LinkedIn being a professional networking site, it simply means that members on LinkedIn are likely going to connect with those whom they share some professional value – be it belonging to a similar profession or having similar or mutually beneficial professional interests.

This means that to be able to touch base with your target audience, you have to belong to relevant groups.

Why you should be using LinkedIn groups

There are five core reasons that would drive you to use LinkedIn groups for your marketing effort:

1. Enhance your credibility – Showing mastery of your core area of competence is important in thought-leadership. This helps to strengthen your Goodwill and thus generate a positive response to your marketing campaign. Sharing relevant content, providing incisive ideas and commenting on latest industry development can help to boost your thought-leadership.

2. Expand the reach of your content – Content marketing is important to your marketing endeavor. LinkedIn groups provide you with an avenue where you can share your content.

3. Generate ideas for new content – With LinkedIn groups, you can learn what attracts attention by learning about the most-talked-about topics. This can help you fine-tune your content strategy.

4. Learn about your target audience – The easiest way to learn your target audience is by being closer to them as much as you can. LinkedIn groups provide such high level of proximity. With proper listening, you can easily tell your audience's desires, needs, challenges, fears, and pain points. This can help you in your entire marketing endeavor right from product design, branding, and delivery.

5. Find the crowd for your next event – You will occasionally require hosting seminars, PR events, and networking events. You would definitely want to reach out to those whom your events can have a significant impact. Inviting members of your group will not only help you gain the required crowd but also enhance your relationship by building stronger bonds.

The advantages of LinkedIn groups to your marketing endeavor

LinkedIn groups can serve your marketing endeavor in various ways. The following are some of the advantages that you gain from LinkedIn groups:

1. Groups let you connect to a thriving community

LinkedIn groups provide some of the best professional communities that you can have on social media. Members are highly committed. This saves you the effort of creating your own community from which to draw potential leads.

2. Groups help in establishing your network

LinkedIn groups help you establish personal connections and networking. You can leverage on this network to boost your marketing effort.

3. They can be used for lead generation

Leads come from the community. Groups help to bring those leads closer to you. Furthermore, you can still draw more leads outside the group through members' connections.

4. Groups can drive traffic to your site

Once you have established a reputable relationship with members of your group, it is much easier to request them to visit your site thus increasing your site's traffic and potential leads.

5. Groups can be used to establish yourself as a thought leader

Within groups, you have the power to generate and foster ideas. This helps to influence people's mindset. When people find your thoughts compelling, they become aligned with your thoughts and as such, you become their thought leader. You can use this thought leadership to persuade them to throw their weight behind your brand.

How to find and join the right group

There are thousands of groups on LinkedIn. It can be a daunting task to find the one which fits your needs. The following steps can help you identify the right group to belong:

- Establish your goal – Be mission-specific when it comes to finding the right group. Having specific goals will help you narrow down your search criteria to only those groups that fit your goal. For example, do you want to find peers, potential customers, or potential vendors?

- Use the right search terms – With your goals in mind, you can define terms to use which will enable the search engine to come with groups that match them.

- Take a lead from those you follow – Find out where the bulk of your followers come from. Most likely, the groups that they come from will have something in common with your needs. Evaluate them and see the ones that you can join

- Read group descriptions – A group's description can enable you to establish what the group is all about. Some groups have specific kind of people that they want to join them. This will help you determine whether the group is right for you or not.

- Gauge the quality of group discussions – Within the shortlist of your potential groups, follow up on their discussions and gauge the quality in terms of relevance, depth level, and engagement

- Join a few of your selected groups – Sometimes the best experience is insider experience. Being in groups will help you to understand their inner workings and your comfort level. If you do not feel comfortable being within a certain group, you can leave it.

- Join groups where your customers and peers are more likely to be – If you want to boost your marketing effort, you would want to associate with groups where your customers are.

- Expand your connections – it is much easier to join a group and receive attention than to be followed by members of that group. Thus, you might need to use LinkedIn Connections Service to grow your following.

How to create a successful LinkedIn Group

If you find out that none of the groups caters for your specific interest, you are free to create your own group. You could find people who have similar interest and need for such a group.

To be able to create a successful LinkedIn group:

1. Pick a topic that resonates with your customers' needs

Your group should focus on a topic that has a natural connection to your brand but not actively promoting your brand or company. For example, if your brand is a fitness gear brand, your topic should be about fitness workout in general rather than your specific brand. This way, your audience will begin to gradually and naturally start connecting with the topic and your brand. This has a more valuable long-term impact than a sales pitch.

2. Create your LinkedIn Group

With the right topic in mind, you can now go ahead and create your LinkedIn group. Simply navigate to your <u>LinkedIn Groups</u> and click on "Create Group". You will be directed to a form to fill in the group details which include Group title, Group logo, description, group rules, and group membership type (standard, or unlisted).

3. Set up message templates

Message templates help to create custom messages that would automatically be sent to people interested in joining your LinkedIn Group.

4. Invite your connections and grow your group

Once you have set up your group, you can now invite your connections to join the group. Also, encourage group members to invite their connections into the group.

5. Start discussions and be active

Make posts, the first being the Welcome Post where you welcome new members to the group, tell them what it is all about and remind them to observe the rules for the good conduct in the group. Start and engage in discussions based on the question-

and-answer format of posts. You need to be actively engaging them and post more since your posts and discussions will set the benchmarks of what you expect from group members.

6. Moderate all posts and remove spam

Moderation helps to ensure that there are no spam posts. Spam posts are a turn-off and will lead to members quitting the group. Set LinkedIn auto-moderation system to flag promotional content.

7. Take advantage of the promotional area

Linked in has a "Promotions" section. This is where you share articles and other kind of content that link back to your site. It is not a place for a sales pitch.

8. Build connections and Follow Up

Keep yourself active in your group through posts, engagement, and moderation. Be respectful of the opinion of other members even if you tend to disagree with them.

How to optimize your opportunities within your group

The following are ways by which you can optimize your opportunities within your group:

- Follow the rules – Observe the group's rules. Learn the group's etiquette and keep observing it.

- Become engaged – Respond to other people's posts and comments. Let it not be all about you.

- Post as an individual, not a company – people like engaging with other people, not entities. People do business with people. This should inform the way you post.

- Stay relevant – Provide content that benefits the group as a whole, not just you. Let the content create value for the group and other members. Self-centeredness turns-off others.

- Avoid regurgitating same content from one group to the other. Some members of your group are also members of some other groups that you belong. If they encounter the same post again in another group, they will be pissed off and this lowers your reputation.

- Be an active, contributing member – Dormancy works against your marketing endeavor.

- Showcase your expertise – Share information, content and ideas about your core area of specialty. Establish yourself as both a thought leader and an expert in your field.

- Take polls and ask questions – Posting a poll and asking questions is the best way to gauge your audience opinion. This not only boosts engagement but also helps you have

the right perspective on them and device appropriate
marketing strategy.

HOW TO USE LINKEDIN ADS

Ads are a very important marketing tool that no firm can afford to ignore. LinkedIn has plenty of unique Ad types that you can use to advance your marketing effort.

To be able to use LinkedIn Ads effectively, the following are the important steps you need to follow:

- Establish your buyer persona
- Determine the right approach to target your buyer persona
- Decide the right Ad(s) to target your buyer persona
- Select your bidding option
- Establish your ad budget
- Launch your Ad

Establish your buyer persona

At the end of it, you want your Ads to convert. This cannot happen if you are not targeting potential buyers. Thus, you need to establish your buyer persona so that you can have targeted Ads. The following are ways to establish your buyer persona.

- List down all traits and demographics of your ideal buyer e.g. age bracket, education level, urbanity, income level, among others

- Speculate about their likely pain points, motivations, and concerns
- You can also use Facebook Audience Insights and Google Trends to determine additional info about your buyer persona

Determine the right approach to target your buyer persona

Once you have established your buyer persona, the next thing to do is to find the right packaging of your Ads in such a manner that will inspire their positive response to your CTA (Call-to-Action)

Decide the right ad(s) to target your buyer persona

Depending on your approach, the following are the types of LinkedIn Ads that you can use:

- LinkedIn Self-Serve Ads
- Sponsored content
- Text Ads
- Sponsored InMail
- LinkedIn Display Ads
- LinkedIn Dynamic Ads

- LinkedIn Marketing Partner Ads
- LinkedIn Video Ads

LinkedIn self-service Ads

LinkedIn allows you to publish your own Ads through its Campaign Manager. You can schedule the campaigns in advance, target your desired audience and be able to get metrics of those who click your Ads including their industry, job function and level of seniority.

Sponsored Content

Sponsored Content is a facility that lets you share posts on your Company Page with a targeted audience on LinkedIn. This is a great feature as it allows you an opportunity to customize your Ads within your content and put it in your most desired way.

Sponsored content helps you to:

- Attract more followers to your Company page
- Extend your content's reach
- Integrate LinkedIn's lead generation forms
- Capture views and clicks on mobile, tablet and desktop

Text Ads

Text Ads are a common form of advertisement online and not necessarily unique to LinkedIn. However, on LinkedIn, they spruced up to include more features such as a desktop-only option feature that lets you have a compelling headline, concise description, and customized eye-catching image.

Text Ads allows you the following benefits:

- A quick start
- Budget-friendly customizations
- Conversion tracking
- Focused target audience based on precision filters

Sponsored InMail

This feature is natively unique to LinkedIn that allows you to deliver personalized messages to a targeted LinkedIn audience through LinkedIn Messenger. It is designed for maximum attention such that the message alerts come when the targets are actively online.

Sponsored InMail can be used to:

- Make personalized invites to events and webinars
- Promote downloadable content such as whitepapers and eBooks

LinkedIn Display Ads

Display Ads are a common mode of online advertisement. LinkedIn has customized Display Ads, which you can buy from your preferred advertising platform, or auction (both private and public). They are highly versatile in terms of multimedia capabilities as you can incorporate text, images, audio, and video for maximum attraction and experience.

You can use Display Ads to:

- To quickly reach out to a wider audience during the initial launch of your campaign
- Strategically locate and expose your campaign to high traffic sources on LinkedIn
- Cut across diverse categories of an audience including thought-leaders, opinion-shapers, influencers, and decision-makers

LinkedIn Dynamic Ads

Dynamic Ads are highly intelligent ads that provide customized Ad message based on the target's behavior. For example, if a prospect is searching for a job vacancy within your industry, the dynamic Ad will customize a message for the prospect regarding a job at your place. Dynamic Ads are highly personalized and customizable.

You can use Dynamic Ads to:

- Reach out to the most influential members of your audience
- Build and cultivate a strong relationship with the targeted audience
- Deliver highly personalized and compelling message to boost the desired action
- Attract specific action through customized CTA
- Widen personalized reach through a wide range of criteria
- Grow a loyal following to your Company's page.

LinkedIn Marketing Partner Ads

These are Ads created by LinkedIn marketing partners. If you feel that you are not confident, or you do not have an in-house team of expert marketers, then you may seek LinkedIn marketing partners to carry out Ads on your behalf. They do have the right experience to deliver Ads as per your expectations.

Video Ads (coming soon)

LinkedIn has been experimenting with video Ads, which are currently in beta release. They are projected for a full launch by the end of the first half of 2018. Like other native LinkedIn Ads, they will be available through LinkedIn's Campaign Manager.

Choose Your Bidding Options

Once you have selected your preferred Ad type, then next step is to choose your bidding option. There are two traditional types of bids:

- CPM (Cost Per Impressions) – This is costing based on impressions (views, exposure) on your Ad. One unit is worth 1000 impressions. Thus, every time the impressions reach 1000, you are billed a certain agreed amount. CPM is ideal when you are targeting brand awareness. Here clicking is not as important as reading the message.

- CPC (Cost per Click) – This is costing based on the number of clicks made on your Ad. CPM is ideal when you are targeting conversion and thus people have to click to make a buy decision.

Establish your ad budget

Budgeting is crucial for your marketing campaign. If you are starting out, it is better to set a daily budget so that you can monitor the performance of your various Ads before deciding on the type of Ads that you are going to promote on a long-term basis. It is only after being assured of the type of Ad that does well that you can set a long-term budget on it. Never assume that the type of Ad that appeals to you most will also be the most appealing to your audience base. Carrying out A/B Testing with a pair of Ads will help you save your budget from being spent on the wrong type of Ad.

Launch and run your ad campaign

You can now go ahead, launch your Ad, and run your Ad campaign. To make a successful launch and Ad campaign, you will need to consider the following steps:

1. Go to <u>Ads</u> platform and select "Create Ad" to launch your Ad. You will be directed to your Member dashboard (Campaign Manager) where you will be required to enter your billing information.
2. Click on the call-to-action (CTA) button to create a campaign. Select the kind of Ad you want to create.
3. Set your Ad's basic parameters These include:
   - Ad's primary language
   - Campaign name
   - Targeted demographic
4. Establish your Ad's media and format - This is now about building your actual Ad based on the parameters. Here you will consider factors such as format, layout, among others. In building the Ad, the following will be required:
   - Ad headline – This is a maximum of 25 characters

- Ad body – This is a maximum of 75 characters. It should be targeted to a specific buyer persona. Its content should be relevant to both the buyer persona and the landing page you are directing them to.
- CTA – Have actionable CTA to boost click-through
- Value – Make a value proposition. The value should be in terms of what the audience benefits by responding to CTA. This could be a special discount, etc. It should also have time value in the sense that it draws urgency to take action.
- Testing – Carry out A/B Testing by using multiple variations of your Ad in each campaign so that you can tell which of them has a higher impact on future campaigns.

5. Target your Ad – Use LinkedIn filtering parameters to target your Ad for the 'right clicks' and maximum impact. This is optional. Specify parameters relevant to your Ad campaign. In this targeting, you can specify:
   - Location
   - Company
   - Job title
   - Member schools
   - Member skills
   - Member groups
   - Gender and age

MONETIZING YOUR LINKEDIN FOLLOWING

Monetization is the reward of every marketing endeavor. You obviously would like to be rewarded for your effort. LinkedIn offers unique monetization opportunities that can be of great benefit to your business. However, being a professional network, it means you have to employ uniquely different marketing and monetization strategy than you would on other social media networks.

Understanding LinkedIn Monetization Strategies

Before you engage in monetization effort, you first need to understand the best approach to LinkedIn monetization. Primarily, LinkedIn monetization is less about content monetization and more about monetization of smart networking. This is radically fundamental.

Content monetization simply means using content as a sales vehicle. It primarily focuses on affiliate marketing, information products, advertising and such like. This is less of a focus when it comes to professional networking where ideas and influence through thought leadership are the primary focus. Nonetheless, this does not necessarily mean that you cannot use content monetization strategies. It simply means that they should be secondary in nature. LinkedIn has a publication feature that can allow you to utilize content monetization.

Understanding LinkedIn Channels

LinkedIn has features that allow you to connect with others, form core interest groups, promote yourself, publish content, and promote products, among others.

The following are the main LinkedIn channels that you can use to advance your monetization endeavors:

- LinkedIn Profiles – LinkedIn profiles are places to showcase yourself, your company, your services or products. You can link each to your personal blog, company website, landing page, respectively.
- Long-form publishing – LinkedIn allows long-form publishing. You can use long-form publishing to provide infographics, thought-provoking multimedia content, among others.
- Groups – Groups provide an excellent opportunity to categorize your audience according to specific interests and criteria. They are a great place for closer and deeper engagement.

- Advertising – LinkedIn, unlike other social media, provides you an opportunity to target your advert to anyone within the network based on a number of filtering options.

How to use your LinkedIn account to monetize your following

LinkedIn is a great place for established brands to make money. There are two phases involved in your monetization endeavor:

- Preparatory phase, and
- Monetization phase

Preparatory phase

In this phase, you are laying a solid groundwork for monetization. You are building the monetization factory. How far you will succeed in the monetization phase depends on how successful you were in the preparatory phase. This is why it is important to spend considerable time in the preparatory phase until you are confident enough that you are ready for take-off to the next phase. Unlike other social media, LinkedIn is not a place for 'hit-and-run' kind of affair. It is not a place for sprinters but marathoners. You have to focus on the long-term.

In this, you need to:

- Build your LinkedIn profile – It is common to have a basic profile like so many that exists on LinkedIn. However, when it comes to monetization, there is more work to be done. First, your profile must be complete. Second, it must be aesthetically appealing (good-looking photo). Third, it must prove compelling value – in terms of great resume (what you have done) evidenced by portfolio (what you have achieved/ your success story).

- Tell a brand story – In this regard, you need to articulate clearly your vision, mission, and the journey so far traveled in terms of accomplished milestones and where you are heading. It should be inspiring enough for your audience to want to be part of your journey.

- Build bonds – This is the core essence of LinkedIn – to create professional networks. However, being connected is one thing and building bonds is another thing. The connection is the first step, which most people on LinkedIn achieve. Building bond is the ultimate step that most do not bother to endeavor. Building bond is about creating that strong affinity, attraction, and ties through a common fabric. You must create something, which people within your network feel connected to, and find it hard to do without it. This could be a great idea, a great value, or a great service.

- Grow your mailing list – Use your connections to grow your mailing list. It is from this mailing list that you can leverage your monetization effort. It is extremely important to growing your mailing list before launching your monetization campaign. This allows your connections to get accustomed to your mailing list for valued services rather than a sales pitch. When you later on introduce measured sales pitch, they will not get offended.

Monetization phase

This is the reaping phase. It is a phase where you direct your focus on making monetary gains from your effort at the preparatory phase.

1. Sell Info Products

You can leverage your LinkedIn following to sell info products. These info products could be white papers, eBooks, reports, webinars, and free training. The following are some of the ways by which you can achieve this:

- Create free content as an invitation to the wider end of your funnel – you can create white papers, eBooks, and reports and free training as a way of subtly proving your

48

product's concept to your audience. Share links to your squeeze page with your connections and groups.

- Connect with influencers in your niche and inspire them to share out your info products.
- Offer discounts to LinkedIn members on your info products – Create special offer code for your new info products and share with your connections and groups
- Invite people to your webinar – Provide free webinars that offer high-value education. You can have a sales pitch within and at the end. People will tend to respond positively as a psychological reward for your great service.
- Take advantage of the Projects Section of your LinkedIn profile to add your new product – This is the only section of your profile that has the room for you to link directly to your website
- Seek reviews of your info products from influential members of your group or connections

2. Sell Physical or Digital Products

You can tactically sell physical or digital products on LinkedIn. The following are some of the ways by which you can do this:

- Exploit the Products Section of your LinkedIn company page to create product listings and clickable banners linked to your landing pages, product demo videos, and 'learn more' pages.

- Take advantage of your LinkedIn summary section to put CTA presentations and commercials.

- Create or get involved in groups whose members are more inclined to buy your products. Present your product as a solution to their unique needs where you find them seeking a solution, which your product can adequately serve.

- Inspire people to click on the 'Recommend' button on your product page. This helps to boost your social proof on LinkedIn

3. Increase Book Sales

LinkedIn, being a professional network where ideas and thoughts are highly encouraged, it follows that books (being nothing but a package of thoughts and ideas) would also be welcomed. However, it is important to ensure that your book is highly targeted to its likely beneficiaries.

To increase your book sales:

- Inform your connections the launching date of your new book. If possible, invite them to the launching event, either physically or through webinars. You can send this information through customized private messages.

- Incorporate your books to the 'Publications" section of your LinkedIn profile. You can link them to your Amazon page or online store for them to click and buy.

- Join groups whose core interests are relevant to the topic of your book. This allows you to discuss the topic and associate your book with the topic. It is an easier way of informing them about your book without appearing to augment a sales pitch. Listen to cues that inform you that the moment is opportune for you to mention your book.

- Create a video summary or trailer of your book. Launch it on your YouTube channel and then insert it as a Media element in the summary section of your LinkedIn profile.

- Request an influential member of your connections to review your book and share it with his/her audience.

- Write a post about your book on your blog and add a LinkedIn share button to the blog post. Click the LinkedIn button to share it with your connections.

- Take advantage of targeted LinkedIn advertisement to reach out the book to a wider audience than your connections. Of course, you will have to use filters to target the right audience.

4. Find Direct Advertisers and Sponsors

In case you are a web publisher or blogger, you may need direct advertisers and sponsors to buy space on your website or blog.

LinkedIn is a good place to find those in need of such services. You can find such opportunities by:

- Taking advantage of LinkedIn's search page to find potential sponsors and advertisers
- Follow-up on advertisers on the LinkedIn footer, sidebar and other areas on the platform. They could be in need of such other places on your website to advertise their products and services
- Reach out to potential companies and make a cold attempt by reaching out their employees on LinkedIn. You can warm up and nurture the connections just as you would nurture a lead.

5. Promote Affiliate Products

If you are an affiliate marketer, LinkedIn is a great opportunity to promote your affiliate products. However, it is important to note that you will have to be more creative than on other platforms as most members tend to perceive affiliate links negatively if not from people they trust and have deeper engagement with. Thus, you have to do more to build a relationship first and leverage that relationship for affiliate marketing.

The following are ways by which you can promote your affiliate products:

- Use sponsored long-form posts to insert your affiliate products links
- Take advantage of the Products Section of your Page to list your affiliate products with relevant affiliate links
- Use LinkedIn's Ad Facility to advertise your affiliate product
- Create your affiliate product's review posts and place them in the Publications section of your LinkedIn profile.
- Request your influential connections to write a review of your affiliate product and let them share it with their connections. Also, do share the same with your groups.
- You can take advantage of your group by sending them emails about latest product reviews, new product launches, discount codes, limited time offers, among other promotional content.
6. Use LinkedIn Advertising.

Advertising is an opportunity for anyone to reach out to a wider audience. You can advertise any of your products and services to reach out your target audience on LinkedIn. However, create one campaign for each of your product or service in order to have a more accurate target.

7. Offer Consultancy Services

LinkedIn is a great place for freelancers and consultants to offer their professional services. The following are some of the ways by which you achieve this:

- Add relevant skills to your LinkedIn profile. This will introduce you to your potential clients by letting them know that you are qualified to offer certain services.
- Utilize the Service Section of your LinkedIn Company page by posting a listing of your services on offer. You can optimize each of the listings by adding banner images with links to your website, video testimonials, and referees.
- Use SEO keywords relevant to your skills to optimize your LinkedIn profile. This will allow discoverability of your skills by those looking for them.
- Use LinkedIn's advanced filtering tools to find groups where your potential clients are likely to be and join in. This way, you can participate in the group discussions, build rapport and introduce your services.
- Watch out for leading questions indicating that someone is in need of your services and grab the chance to lead the person to your services.
- Link-up with those who offer complimentary services and join their groups. For example, if you are an editor, you

may need to link up with freelance writers; if you offer plumbing services, you may link up with Home and Office building contractors; if you are an SEO expert, link up with web developers.

8. Get Hired

Finding jobs and being hired is the traditional function of LinkedIn that continues to remain relevant over time. It is a place where jobseekers expose themselves to potential recruiters. The following are the ways by which you can boost your chances of being hired on LinkedIn:

- Complete your personal profile and make it up to date with your latest skills and achievements.
- Take advantage of the Summary section of your LinkedIn profile to express your passion, showcase your accomplishments, and prove what you are ready to deliver to your potential employer.
- If you are targeting a company for a job, follow the company's page and deeply engage with it by commenting on their posts. Also, join groups in which the company's senior-most staffs relevant to your field are. Keep checking their Career's tab and the Job section of the company's page for likely openings, which you can respond to them.
- Premium account for job seekers is a great feature that you should exploit, as it will push your applications on top list

to make it stand out. The premium icon on it will also help to accentuate its case.

GROWING YOUR LINKEDIN FOLLOWING

A large LinkedIn following simply means a wider opportunity for exposure and a greater lead potential. Thus, it is important for you to grow your LinkedIn following to optimize your marketing effort.

The following are some of the ways to grow your LinkedIn following:

1. Leverage your LinkedIn profile and company page

Your personal profile and company page are great tools to increase your LinkedIn following. You can optimize these by:

- Making sure that your LinkedIn profile is complete and up-to-date with the latest information.
- Optimizing the first 150 characters of your page description for SEO and click-through. It is the first 156 characters that will be displayed on the SERP.
- Having a catchy image on your company's home page to attract visitors' attention.
- Having a QR code on your business card to direct people to your page. Also, include your page's link on your business card.

- Posting your page updates during peak hours such as Morning or Midday on Monday to Friday. This will increase impact on viewership.

- Having multiple showcase pages on your profile each pointing to a particular dimension of your company including departments, product categories, and corporate social responsibility, among others.

- Using your company page as your current place of work. This will automatically cause your logo to be displayed on your personal page, which increases the chances of a click-through.

- Using LinkedIn Connect to synchronize all your contacts on LinkedIn. Request new connects to follow your page.

- Assigning several trusted administrators to your page. Encourage the administrators to post engaging content on your page and share updates with their connections.

- Naming your page using your business full name. This is a way to market your business and create brand awareness. More people who know your business but do not know your company page or personal profile will easily discover you and connect. This will also enhance your ranking on Google search engine.

- Posting your job vacancies on your page. This will increase your page following as potential job seekers will be on the lookout

- Letting your LinkedIn Page link be part of your group signature rather than your web page. This is much easier for your connections to reach without having to leave LinkedIn.

2. Leverage your company employees

- Encourage your employees to join LinkedIn and add your page as their workplace. This automatically makes them your followers and encourages their followers to join you.

- Encourage your employees to actively and positively engage with your page's content. This is a good social proof of your page to other followers.

3. Leverage your content

- Make sure that your page is not a skeleton before requesting for followers. Let them find enough content to keep them occupied, engaged and knowledgeable of what your page is all about.

- Take advantage of LinkedIn Pulse to encourage comments and shares on each post.

- Aim at least five posts per week to keep your presence felt and your followers engaged. The more frequent you post (not compromising on the quality or overwhelming your readers) the more reach you attain.

- Optimize your content through lists to amplify reactions. Lists, especially "the best-of" lists help to boost amplification by close to 40% (according to LinkedIn).

- Take advantage of the images to attract attention. Make sure that your post has at least one relevant, high quality and attractive image.

- Use your page to share inspiring company news. Most professionals are on LinkedIn to eavesdrop on latest company news.

- Provide industry-related insights to attract more following. This is what most professionals are on LinkedIn for.

- Share useful content with your followers. They will greatly appreciate this extra service. Furthermore, you will be able to gauge their interest using such shared content and thus calibrate yours to the same wavelength.

- Be an early listener to the trending topics so that you become among the first to offer breaking insights.

- Provide credible and valuable links within your content. When you do this persistently, your followers will grow a habit of looking up for the links to click and share with their connections. This will help you to earn new connections from their sharing.

- Market your LinkedIn platform. You can do this by creating a blog post about some unique feature or unique connections that need to be followed on LinkedIn (e.g. 10 Professional Financial Advisors on LinkedIn". This will not only increase traffic to your blog, excite more connections, but also improve your page rank on search engines as the search engines may pick a part of your blog post as a LinkedIn keyword (e.g. "Financial Advisors on LinkedIn".

- Do not forget to include CTA at the end of your blog post requesting readers to follow you on LinkedIn.

4. **Leverage your other social media networks and online assets**

- Add LinkedIn button to all your online assets including blogs and web pages.

- Add your company's LinkedIn Follow button to your website and blog

- Use your other online marketing channels such as social media channels (Facebook, Twitter, YouTube, etc) chatting platforms (such Whatsapp, Skype, etc) and emails to increase your LinkedIn page visibility.

- Insert a link to your LinkedIn page in your email signature

- Add your company's LinkedIn widget to your website's sidebar. This will stream relevant information about your company and thus encourage click-through. It also has a Follow button to encourage following of your company's LinkedIn page.

- Share videos on your YouTube channel with your LinkedIn followers. This boosts engagement and shares which attracts a new following. According to LinkedIn, videos create twice as many reactions (comments, shares, etc) compared to posts without videos.

- Guest blog and make sure that you insert a link to your LinkedIn company page in your bio on the guest blog post you make.

- Take advantage of SEO to optimize your LinkedIn pages for searchability. Make sure you include relevant keywords in your long-form posts and your page description.

5. **Leverage your engagements**

- Have active engagement in LinkedIn groups. Share your thoughts and insights regarding your industry and profession. Build thought-leadership around this core area. You will gain more trust and following as an industry expert with a lot to offer.

- Make your current connections excited before attempting to grow more. Otherwise, you may achieve short-term success and long-term loss as more connections exit.

6. Leverage the LinkedIn tools and features

- Keep attention to your LinkedIn's content marketing score. This score will inform you of what percentage of your following is being reached by your content marketing campaign. The score also has metrics that enable you to know how you are performing against competition within your industry. This grants you an opportunity to strategize and improve your content marketing campaign effort.

- Keep your eyes on LinkedIn analytics and performance metrics with regard to how your posts are doing in terms of inspiring your audience. You can then emulate your best performing posts as your standard. This is also a good way to gauge your followers' core interests and match strategy towards them.

7. Leverage your LinkedIn group and existing following

- Inspire your connections to follow your page and share it out with their own connections

- Make more connections by following more pages. The more expansive your network becomes, the greater the potential of growing your page's following.

- Identify your complementary businesses in your industry and follow them. Engage with them and share their content. They are more likely to return the favor and join you in wider partnership as you have mutual interest.

- Identify those members that appear to be good at consuming content and connect with them. They are more likely to consume your long-form content and establish deeper connections with you. They are also more likely to summarize key points on your behalf as they share it out with their connections. Encourage those who show positive response to do so.

- Take advantage of questions to raise your audience interest and gauge their sentiments. According to LinkedIn, you are likely going to get 50% more comments on posts with questions.

- Create or Join an industry-related LinkedIn group. Share relevant content and valuable information as a means of introducing an engaging discussion.

- Keep self-promoting content to a minimum. Employ Pareto's 80/20 rule such that 80% of your content should be non-promotional content while only 20% should be promotional.

- Segment your followers based on their key interests so that you can have more targeted posts that raise engagement. This will encourage a higher level of engagement, more shares with their connections sharing similar interests and the net result will be more following.

AUTOMATING LINKEDIN INCOME

Automation is the best way to scale up your LinkedIn monetization effort. Without automation, you will be dwarfed by the overwhelming amount of work that you need to do just to maintain your current status, leave alone growing.

The advantage of automating your LinkedIn Income:

- Cost cutting – With LinkedIn income automation, you are able to cut costs in terms of time and money. In some core functions, using automation tools can achieve you much more than what you would achieve from hiring 20 people.

- Structured approach – Humans tend to be erratic and unstructured depending on many biological factors. However, automation tools will be more structured as they are not susceptible to human biases. This way, you can be able to get a more precise outcome.

- Larger-than-life presence – Automating certain LinkedIn functions such as visiting your followers' profiles, making personalized emails can make you appear larger-than-life.

Automation tools can work 24/7, unlike a human being. The can also visit multiple profiles at the same time.

Popular LinkedIn Automation Tools

1. LinkedIn Sales Navigator – This is a relationship-building tool that helps you identify potential leads through its recommendation mechanism and helps you to draw your leads ever closer to the sales funnel.

2. Rapportive – It gathers data from LinkedIn profiles social media network accounts and web URLs to provide you crucial information about leads' contacts and other important personal details.

3. LinkedIn Plugins – These are plugins that help to enhance your LinkedIn account functionality. Some of the popular LinkedIn plugins include;
   - Company Profile
   - Follow Company
   - Company Insider
   - Alumni Tool
   - Member Profile
   - LinkedIn AutoFill
   - Share

4. LinkedIn Small Business Center – This is a LinkedIn in-built facility dedicated to helping small businesses grow. It helps you to establish a brand presence, connect with the

target audience and use content marketing to engage with them.

5. Crystal – Crystal is a profiling tool that reviews LinkedIn profile and provides insight into the person's personality. This helps you decide on the best way to approach a given prospect. As such, it is a buyer persona's automation tool. When you want to draft email and other communication, Crystal will recommend to you the best approach based on the identified persona.

6. LeadFuze – This is a leads prospecting tool. It helps you generate a list of potential leads. You can use its lead builder to send personalized emails and follow-ups automatically.

7. SalesLoft Prospector - This tool enables you to personalize your communication based on email tracking, use built-in sales dialer to increase sales performance, and gather incisive analytics.

8. Outro – It uses "relationship strength algorithm" to help you establish qualified leads.

9. Salestools.io - This download your LinkedIn lists to Excel. With the Excel, you can easily manipulate the data to suit your particular need such as ranking prospects in order of

importance. You can also use the tool to extend personal outreach messages and track your leads activities.

10. eLink Pro – This tool automates profile visitation. Most of the time, people visit your profile and connect with you based on your visit to their own profiles. The more profiles you visit the higher the likelihood of being visited back. This tool does the visitation work for you.

11. Discoverly – This tool provides you with information about your leads' other social media activities so that you are able to know them better.

12. Guru – This tool helps to build a profile of potential leads by finding and availing data such as prospect's competitors, prospect's current customers that work in the same industry, sales data related to the prospect's industry, among others.

13. FollowingLike – This tool helps you manage not only LinkedIn but also multiple social media accounts.

14. eGrabber – This tool helps to find missing information about your potential prospects such as emails and phone numbers of your LinkedIn connections. It does this by extracting this data from various other sources online including other networking sites and online directories.

15. ProTop – This tool helps you to search the right buyer persona and generate leads. It automatically visits profiles

of LinkedIn users that match your set criteria and helps to drive attention and traffic to your profile.

16. InBoardPro- This tool helps you to manage multiple LinkedIn accounts, generate leads, and get right candidates for recruitment.

17. Scout – This marketing automation tool is used to carry out sales prospecting. With it, you are able to get personal contact information of your top LinkedIn leads.

18. Nimble – This is a CRM tool. It uses Relationship Intelligence to enable you to make real-time discovery of detailed profiles and automate social profile matching.

19. LinkedIn Dominator – Helps you to add connections based on keywords.

Outsourcing as part of the automation process

Automation tools cannot handle all the human functions. Roles such as responding to posts and comments require a human touch. Engagement is one key area that you will need not to surrender to automation tools as you are likely going to get negative results. However, due to automation of other functions, the volume of engagement requirements flares up to such a level that you cannot manage alone. You will need to hire someone to help you carry out the engagement function. Luckily, many trained and experienced virtual assistants exist who can do this work on your behalf. Outsourcing some of the engagement work to virtual assistants would help you complement what automation tools are doing.

You can easily get freelance virtual assistants from Upwork, Freelancer, People Per Hour and Fiverr, among other freelancing sites.

CONCLUSION

Thank you for acquiring this guide and reading it to the end.

It is my sincere hope that information provided in this guide has enabled you to use LinkedIn B2B marketing to generate qualified prospects and obtain clients. It is also my sincere hope that you have been inspired enough to recommend this guide to your friends and colleagues so that they too can obtain a copy of it and that it can help them succeed in their LinkedIn income generation endeavor.

Again, thank you for acquiring this guide.

Have good luck!